100X

Prepare The Soil
Protect The Seed
Produce More Than Enough

The ARK Network

If you have not set up a free account on our network please do so now. Here you will find community, devotionals and all of the ARK courses.

You can go through this workbook on your own or with a group.
All of the pre-recorded videos are available

arkidentity.com

LIST OF COURSES

100X: Prepare, Protect, Produce

Identity Through The Trinity: Who is God and How does He see you?

The Way: The Essentials of The Christian Faith

The Bridge: Prophetic Evangelism - Living on mission

Freedom: The New Wine Skin

Sabbath: A Guide to New Covenant Rest - Back to the garden

Come To The Table: Hospitality Evangelism

DNA: Exponential Discipleship - How to make disciples who multiply

Sacred: Our Identity Together - The Power of Marriage

SE7EN: The Spirit of God and the Lamp within you

The Fear of the Lord: Pathway To Joy

Ready Set Go!: 40 Days Through The Book of Joshua

www.arkidentity.com

ABOUT THE ARK IDENTITY

The Ark Identity: Fully Knowing God ~ God knowing you!

> *Now this is eternal life: that they know you, the only true God, and Jesus Christ, whom you have sent.* **- John 17:3 NIV**

The ARK Identity equips followers of Jesus to know their true identity and hear God's voice. We accomplish this through a series of 6 week trainings that expose the lies we believe and reveal the reality of Christ in His finished work. Our goal is exponential multiplication of trainers and facilitators who can disciple others in communities around the world.

> *And the things you have heard me say in the presence of many witnesses entrust to reliable people who will also be qualified to teach others.* **- 2 Timothy 2:2 NIV**

Pillars of The ARK

- To personally hear God's voice through His word and Spirit
- To know our true Identity through experiencing the Trinity
- To be disciples who make disciples

THE ARK IDENTITY

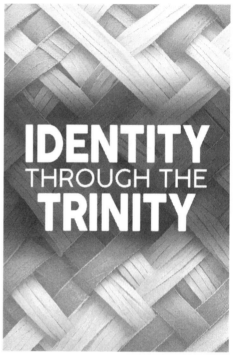

Prepare your heart for spiritual transformation.

Knowing God and who God says you are.

4 SESSIONS

3D EXPERIENCE

DISCIPLESHIP TRACK

God is speaking but can you hear Him clearly?

These are the essentials of the faith we proclaim.

3 SESSIONS

6 SESSIONS

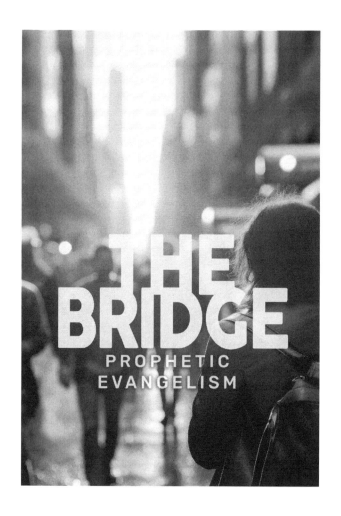

Living on mission everyday of your Christian life.

TRAINING AND MISSION TRIP

3D.ARKIDENTITY.COM/BRIDGE

TABLE OF CONTENTS

Session One: Prepare The Soil

Can you identify the areas of life that are hindering the word of God from taking root in your heart? Jesus gave us the parable of the four soils so we could identify the condition of our hearts and surrender to his transformation. Only the good soil produces a harvest of thirty, sixty, or even a hundred times what has been planted!

Session Two: Protect The Seed

God has given you tools to protect what He has planted in you. Discover the protective power of community, consistency, and consecration. These three tools will safeguard your spiritual growth and multiplication. By actively partnering with God in these areas, you'll be equipped to navigate life's challenges and temptations, and to produce a bountiful harvest for His kingdom.

Session Three: The Three Tests

God uses tests to reveal your true identity. Learn to discern between God's tests, which lead to growth and the crown of life, and the enemy's tests, which seek to expose and remind you of your past. This session will equip you to stand firm in your identity as God's beloved, patiently endure life's challenges, and embrace the transformative power of God's testing.

Session Four: Produce 100X

Discover how the seed of Christ within you can multiply beyond what you could imagine. The fruit of the Holy Spirit in your life will allow you to sow the Seed of Christ in the lives of others. By the end of this session, you will be equipped to produce a harvest of righteousness and praise that will spring up before all the nations. It's time to produce 100x.

GET READY

Before jumping into the ARK courses or a discipleship relationship, it is highly important that you prepare the soil of your heart to receive the revelation that is about to be sown into your life. Jesus teaches this concept in Mark chapter 4 with a parable about four kinds of soil. Three of these soils are unable to multiply the seed at all because the soil was uncultivated and as a result the seed was wasted.

Ways you can prepare?

- What responsibilities could distract you while you are at a 3D Experience? Work on these ahead of time or delegate these to someone else. Communicate with your family how they can help.

- Who would commit to praying for you as you grow? Intercessory prayer is powerful. Our prayer team is praying for you by name as well.

- Fast before the experience. Maybe you fast from screen time (phone and TV). We find that a water fast is the most powerful form of fasting and can make us more aware of God's presence in every moment.

- Watch this entire series. The purpose of this video series is to help you identify areas of your life that will hinder the word of God from taking root in your heart.

Ask God!

How do you want me to prepare for this experience?

What do you sense God is saying to you?

Session One

PREPARE THE SOIL

Then Jesus said to them, "If you can't understand the meaning of this parable, how will you understand all the other parables? **- Mark 4:13**

Warm Up Question
What is a parable?

___

___

___

SEED AND SOIL

Mark 4 (NLT)

> 3 "Listen! A farmer went out to plant some seed. 4 As he scattered it across his field, some of the seed fell on a footpath, and the birds came and ate it. 5 Other seed fell on shallow soil with underlying rock. The seed sprouted quickly because the soil was shallow. 6 But the plant soon wilted under the hot sun, and since it didn't have deep roots, it died. 7 Other seed fell among thorns that grew up and choked out the tender plants so they produced no grain. 8 Still other seeds fell on fertile soil, and they sprouted, grew, and produced a crop that was thirty, sixty, and even a hundred times as much as had been planted!" 9 Then he said, "Anyone with ears to hear should listen and understand."

Who is the farmer?
God's ministers are the farmers scattering seed across the world (field).

What is the seed?
The seed is the word of God. (The revelation of Jesus Christ.)

Where is the soil?
The soils represent the hearts of people and the condition of their hearts.

> **Mark 4:13** Then Jesus said to them, "If you can't understand the meaning of this parable, how will you understand all the other parables? 14 The farmer plants seed by taking God's word to others.

You are about to receive a lot of seed. All throughout the discipleship journey you are going to be immersed in conversations and encounters that will break up the hard places, cut back the thorns, and pull out the unhealthy debris that will hinder growth. The best thing you can do is surrender to the process, yield to the experience, and say yes to what God wants to do in your life.

THE FOUR SOILS

As we go through this study, be honest with yourself. What kind of soil are you? This is not intended to bring shame in your life, but to help you realize the condition of your heart and then ask God and His people for help to be transformed into good soil. He did this in my life. And if He could do it for me, He can do it again for you and those around you.

_____ Ground (Pathway) No entry

> **Mark 4:15** *The seed that fell on the footpath represents those who hear the message, only to have Satan come at once and take it away.*

Some people have hearts that are unable to receive God's word at all. It's like casting seed on concrete. The seed is exposed and is immediately snatched up by Satan or "birds" as mentioned in the original parable. This ground needs to be dug up, turned, tilled and cultivated.

> *I said, 'Plant the good seeds of righteousness,*
> *and you will harvest a crop of love.*
> *Plow up the hard ground of your hearts,*
> *for now is the time to seek the Lord,*
> *that he may come*
> *and shower righteousness upon you.'* **- Hosea 10:12 NLT**

_____ Ground (Rocky places) Surface level

> **Mark 4:16** *The seed on the rocky soil represents those who hear the message and immediately receive it with joy. 17 But since they don't have deep roots, they don't last long. They fall away as soon as they have problems or are persecuted for believing God's word.*

Some hearts look good on the surface, but they have solid ground a few inches down. They can receive the word with lots of potential, but their environment won't allow long term growth. Without roots a plant will never produce. Without godly community the word of God will not be able to grow.

> *The sluggard will not plow during the planting season,*
> *so at harvest time he asks for grain but has nothing.*
> **- Proverbs 20:4 NET**

_____ Ground (Uncultivated) Cluttered

> **Mark 4:18** *The seed that fell among the thorns represents others who hear God's word, 19 but all too quickly the message is crowded out by the worries of this life, the lure of wealth, and the desire for other things, so no fruit is produced.*

This person is so consumed by finances, success, concerns, and the lust of the eyes that they have no room for God. Even as the word is being released they are thinking about other things. What's for lunch? How am I going to pay that bill? When is this going to be over?

> *The one who works his field will have plenty of food,*
>
> *but whoever chases daydreams lacks sense.*
>
> **- Proverbs 12:11 NET**

_____ Soil (Yielded) Ready to produce

> **Mark 4:20** *And the seed that fell on good soil represents those who hear and accept God's word and produce a harvest of thirty, sixty, or even a hundred times as much as had been planted!"*

This person is like a sponge. They soak up the word, sit in it, squeeze it out on other sponges and come back for more. They have a heart of multiplication. One seed will produce millions of seeds and they will eventually become one of the farmers sowing into the field.

> **Mark 4:26** *Jesus also said, "The Kingdom of God is like a farmer who scatters seed on the ground. 27 Night and day, while he's asleep or awake, the seed sprouts and grows, but he does not understand how it happens. 28 The earth produces the crops on its own. First a leaf blade pushes through, then the heads of wheat are formed, and finally the grain ripens. 29 And as soon as the grain is ready, the farmer comes and harvests it with a sickle, for the harvest time has come."*

What kind of soil are you?

How can we prepare the soil of our lives if we don't understand what kind of soil we are? Maybe we need the eyes of someone we trust who can observe our hearts and help us determine what kind of soil we are. Do you know? And once you know we can apply what is needed so we can be the kind of soil that produces 100X.

HEART CONDITIONING

Break it up

> *This is what the Lord says to the people of Judah and Jerusalem:*
> *"Plow up the hard ground of your hearts!*
>   *Do not waste your good seed among thorns.*
> *- Jeremiah 4:3 NLT*

Let's be honest, some people have hardened hearts that need conditioning before they are able to receive what is about to be sown. The word says to plow up the hard ground. Plowing is not a feel-good thing. It's hard work, it looks messy and it requires submission. A hardened heart that is willing to yield to the plow, that's someone we can work with. But a hardened heart that thinks they know it all, that's someone who is not ready for the seed just yet.

Soften with water

> *You take care of the earth and water it,*
>   *making it rich and fertile.*
> *The river of God has plenty of water;*
>   *it provides a bountiful harvest of grain,*
>   *for you have ordered it so.*
> *10 You drench the plowed ground with rain,*
>   *melting the clods and leveling the ridges.*
> *You soften the earth with showers*
>   *and bless its abundant crops. - Psalm 65:9-10 NLT*

The rain of God's love can soften any heart. Before you plant the seed of God's word, drench that person in His love. It is the goodness of God that leads men to change their ways and turn to God. Maybe you sense that you might have a hardened heart towards God's word and His people. Ask yourself... Am I missing out on love? Allow the rain of God's love to wash over you now even in this moment.

Pull the stones

What about those who appear as good soil only to have bedrock a few inches below the surface. This soil also needs to be plowed, broken up and cleaned of the stones that will hinder long term growth. This takes time and obedience from both the person with the rocky heart and the farmer who is tending to the ground.

Cutback the overgrowth

O people of Judah and Jerusalem,
surrender your pride and power.
Change your hearts before the Lord,
or my anger will burn like an unquenchable fire
because of all your sins. - Jeremiah 4:4 NLT

In the NASB version of the bible this verse says…

"Circumcise yourselves to the Lord

And remove the foreskins of your hearts,"

Ouch! That is a serious word. In farming terms, cutback the areas of your life that are hindering good growth. Surrender doing things your way. Acknowledge that you may be desiring things in this world that will choke out the word of God in your life. Pride and personal power are thorns that will hold you back from producing in God's Kingdom.

Becoming Good Soil

"The rain and snow come down from the heavens
and stay on the ground to water the earth.
They cause the grain to grow,
producing seed for the farmer
and bread for the hungry.
11 It is the same with my word.
I send it out, and it always produces fruit.
It will accomplish all I want it to,
and it will prosper everywhere I send it.
12 You will live in joy and peace.
The mountains and hills will burst into song,
and the trees of the field will clap their hands!
- Isaiah 55:10-12 NLT

God's word can show up in many ways and with many purposes. Some words are released to correct us in our ways, while other words are meant to plant, and yet others are to fertilize or water what has been planted. In all of these purposes, we must hold on to the fact that His word will accomplish what it was sent out for. His word will not return void. This is good news for us.

What role do you play in the transformation of your own heart?

THE CROWN OF ABUNDANCE

> *When Isaac planted his crops that year, he harvested a hundred times more grain than he planted, for the Lord blessed him. He became a very rich man, and his wealth continued to grow.* **- Genesis 26:12 -13 NLT**

Here's a promise. God wants His word to multiply in you. Because of this promise, we can stand on the truth that there is no soil (no heart condition) that can't be transformed. God can turn the hardest of hearts into good soil in a moment. He can cut back all of the distractions and worries. He can clean and fertilize our hearts for planting. He will get what He desires in us. His desire is to crown us with an abundant life. Let's look more at Psalm 65.

> *11 You crown the year with a bountiful harvest;*
> *even the hard pathways overflow with abundance.*
> *12 The grasslands of the wilderness become a lush pasture,*
> *and the hillsides blossom with joy.*
> *13 The meadows are clothed with flocks of sheep,*
> *and the valleys are carpeted with grain.*
> *They all shout and sing for joy!* **- Psalm 65:11-13 NLT**

This should leave you encouraged and abounding in hope. Even the hard ground will overflow. Even the wilderness will become lush. Our job is to remain surrendered. Be still and know that He is God and you are His beloved child. He knows the condition of your heart and what needs to happen so that you might produce 100X.

Let's pray for supernatural grace to prepare our hearts fir the seed that is coming!

Notes

Guard your heart above all else,

for it determines the course of your life.

— **Proverbs 4:23 NLT**

Session Two

PROTECT THE SEED

And the peace of God, which surpasses all comprehension, will guard your hearts and minds in Christ Jesus. **- Philippians 4:7 NASB**

Warm Up Questions
You've made an investment into a business.
What are some ways you would protect your investment?

_____

_____

_____

INVEST AND PROTECT

You have invested lots of resources into a business. Naturally, you would be upset if someone broke in and stole merchandise or equipment. Well this is no different. God has invested seed in your heart. And to God, you are a garden worth protecting. We know Satan is going to attempt to steal, kill and destroy what has been planted. But God has specific things that we can do to protect the seed.

The thief's purpose is to steal and kill and destroy. My purpose is to give them a rich and satisfying life. **- John 10:10 NLT**

Don't be naive, we have an enemy who roams around pretending to be a lion and looking for someone to devour. The enemy will come and attack the seed in various ways. My job is to make sure that you are well equipped and surrounded by His protection as you multiply what has been given to you.

Did you receive a revelation from God? Did you let go of lies and replace them with God's truth? What do you do when the enemy tries to remind you who you used to be? Did you receive healing in your body? What if the enemy tries to reinjure you or bring your symptoms back? What do you do when the enemy starts to tempt you the same way that was working before? You see what I'm getting at right?

Catch all the foxes, those little foxes, before they ruin the vineyard of love, for the grapevines are blossoming!

- Song of Songs 2:15 NLT

What are the foxes?
The foxes are anything that brings chaos into the garden and destroys the crop. And when the foxes come, will they find easy access to your heart? Or will they find a fence of protection?

What are the foxes in your life and how will you protect the garden?

_____

_____

_____

_____

Let's discuss!

THE THREE C'S OF PROTECTION

Community

God has never been alone. Ever! And since you are made in their image you were never meant for isolation. If you are connected to a community, pursue a greater connection. And If you don't have a community that you are connected to we want to help you find it. In community, we help remind one another who we are in Christ. We help protect one another from attacks of the enemy. And we help cover one another in prayer. Community is the number one thing that you can do to protect the seed.

> *Brothers and sisters, even if a person is caught in any wrongdoing, you who are spiritual are to restore such a person in a spirit of gentleness; each one looking to yourself, so that you are not tempted as well. 2 Bear one another's burdens, and thereby fulfill the law of Christ.* **- Galatians 6:1-2 NASB**

Consistency

You have just been immersed in God's word and saturated in His presence. This is not a one time event. It's a way of life. I need His Word in my life everyday. I don't have to read His word, I need to. I don't worship God out of obligation, I need to worship in order to survive and live in constant overflow. Consistency is key. Look back at the scriptures and lessons in the workbook. Dig into the questions again. Ask him again "God when you look at me what do you see?"

> *But He answered and said, "It is written: 'Man shall not live on bread alone, but on every word that comes out of the mouth of God.'"* **- Matthew 4:4 NASB**

Consecration

This is a powerful word that simply means to be set apart for a Holy purpose. After an ARK Training, it's important that you don't return back to life as usual. Protect your eyes and ears from the media and influences that will not reinforce your Identity through the Trinity. Maybe this means there are certain people in your life that need to honor some boundaries you put up. I bet there are some behaviors that can't continue in your life with this fresh identity perspective. It's time to be set apart for a holy purpose and never look back.

> *Therefore, ridding yourselves of all filthiness and all that remains of wickedness, in humility receive the word implanted, which is able to save your souls.* **- James 1:21 NASB**

PROTECT YAH NECK

Jesus is the head and we are His body. As the head, He wants to set up a fence of protection. Will you allow Him to set this up for your protection?

1. Surrender to the community - Allow His Body to protect you as God intended.

> *Be of the same mind toward one another; do not be haughty in mind, but associate with the lowly. Do not be wise in your own estimation.* **- Romans 12:16 NASB**

2. Consume His word consistently - Allow His promises to be your provision.

> *Now these people were more noble-minded than those in Thessalonica, for they received the word with great eagerness, examining the Scriptures daily to see whether these things were so.* **- Acts 17:11 NASB**

3. Separate yourself from the world - Allow Jesus to be your Priest.

> *Therefore, if anyone cleanses himself from these things, he will be an implement for honor, sanctified, useful to the Master, prepared for every good work.* **- 2 Timothy 2:21 NASB**

Introspective

What are your weak spots?

_____

_____

What are practical ways you can partner with God in each area?

_____

_____

Notes

Count it all joy, my brothers, when you meet trials of various kinds, for you know that the testing of your faith produces steadfastness. And let steadfastness have its full effect, that you may be perfect and complete, lacking in nothing.

- James 1:2-4 ESV

Session Three

THE THREE TESTS

In this you greatly rejoice, even though now for a little while, if necessary, you have been distressed by various trials, so that the proof of your faith, being more precious than gold which perishes though tested by fire, may be found to result in praise, glory, and honor at the revelation of Jesus Christ; **- 1 Peter 1:7-8 NASB**

Warm Up Question
What is one way that God tests you?

TEST FOR SUCCESS

I remember in High School I used to hate tests. But here I am as a man who understands that a good teacher will not test you on something you have not been taught. Good teachers test you to prove that what they taught has become understanding. However, a bad teacher will test you to expose things you do not know. They will test you for failure. The same is true spiritually.

> *Dear brothers and sisters, when troubles of any kind come your way, consider it an opportunity for great joy. 3 For you know that when your faith is tested, your endurance has a chance to grow. 4 So let it grow, for when your endurance is fully developed, you will be perfect and complete, needing nothing.* **- James 1:2-4 NLT**

When I had my first real encounter with the Holy Spirit, the enemy immediately sent people who wanted to challenge my experience. They said "That's not real. The Bible was stolen from the ancient Egyptians." There was a moment where I began to doubt my experience, but deep down I knew what happened and I could not deny that God had transformed my heart. The enemy uses tests to expose and remind you of the old you. But God will use tests to reveal who you truly are.

> *God blesses those who patiently endure testing and temptation. Afterward they will receive the crown of life that God has promised to those who love him.* **- James 1:12 NLT**

These two words keep sticking out to me; "patiently endure". Cultivation is a process that cannot be rushed. We can find ways to speed up the process, but that doesn't always produce the best results. Taking a hardened heart through a conditioning process to become good soil can take time. Likewise, planting seeds in the ground and faithfully caring for that crop takes months before others can enjoy the fruit of your life. Remember this is about consistently making small acts of obedience that lead up to a life of massive transformation.

Even Jesus was tested by the enemy when He fasted from food and water in the wilderness for 40 days. Jesus had just received the baptism of the Holy Spirit and the declaration of His Father spoken over Him in front of all the Jews standing at the Jordan River. Do you remember what God said over Jesus when He was baptized?

"Behold, My Beloved Son in whom I am well pleased."

THREE TEMPTATIONS

Immediately after this public declaration Jesus is led by the Holy Spirit into the wilderness to fast. After 40 days, here comes Satan. What does Satan mean? Satan literally means the accuser. He thought he could expose Jesus but in the process he ended up being exposed as a coward and a liar.

Matthew 4:1

Then Jesus was led up by the Spirit into the wilderness to be tempted by the devil. 2 And after He had fasted for forty days and forty nights, He then became hungry. 3 And the tempter came and said to Him, "If You are the Son of God, command that these stones become bread." 4 But He answered and said, "It is written: 'Man shall not live on bread alone, but on every word that comes out of the mouth of God.'"

5 Then the devil *took Him along into the holy city and had Him stand on the pinnacle of the temple, 6 and he *said to Him, "If You are the Son of God, throw Yourself down; for it is written: 'He will give His angels orders concerning You';

and 'On their hands they will lift You up,
So that You do not strike Your foot against a stone.'"
7 Jesus said to him, "On the other hand, it is written: 'You shall not put the Lord your God to the test.'"

8 Again, the devil *took Him along to a very high mountain and *showed Him all the kingdoms of the world and their glory; 9 and he said to Him, "All these things I will give You, if You fall down and worship me." 10 Then Jesus *said to him, "Go away, Satan! For it is written: 'You shall worship the Lord your God, and serve Him only.'" 11 Then the devil *left Him; and behold, angels came and began to serve Him.

Temptation	Object	The Lie	Area of Life	Part of Being
#1				
#2				
#3				

THE MISSING WORD

You are of your father the devil, and you want to do the desires of your father. He was a murderer from the beginning, and does not stand in the truth because there is no truth in him. Whenever he tells a lie, he speaks from his own nature, because he is a liar and the father of lies. - **John 8:44 NASB**

Satan comes to Jesus and says...

"If you are the Son of God...?"

Is this what The Father calls Jesus?
What does the Father call Jesus in Matthew 3 when He was baptized?

     Satan, the accuser, is ok with you believing you are a son or daughter of God. That doesn't bother him at all. You can be a rejected son, a neglected son, a broken son, a hungry son, a prideful son, an abused son and the list goes on. The one thing that Satan does not want you to believe is that you are God's beloved. Satan will never, ever call you beloved. In fact he hates this title and he will do whatever it takes to make you feel unloved.
     If we are going to protect the seed of Christ in us. The number one thing we can do is remain unshakable in our identity as God's beloved children. You may feel unloved. You may feel a lot of things throughout this life but we walk by faith and not by sight. By faith I accept my God given identity as a beloved son of God. And I refuse to allow the enemy to intimidate me into believing his lies and handing over my harvest.

I need you to get up and get ready to make a declaration.

On three, shout this out.

"I am God's beloved!"

Introspective

When the enemy comes to test your seed, will you try to prove yourself to others? Or stand on this new identity that God has declared over your life?

_____
_____
_____
_____
_____
_____
_____
_____
_____
_____

who, as He already existed in the form of God, did not consider equality with God something to be grasped, but emptied Himself...

Session Four

PRODUCE 100X

But the fruit of the Spirit is love, joy, peace, patience, kindness, goodness, faithfulness, 23 gentleness, self-control; against such things there is no law. **- Galatians 5:22-23 NASB**

Warm Up Question
What fruit of the Holy Spirit are you producing the most of?

A TREE OF IT'S OWN KIND

> *The earth produced vegetation, plants yielding seed according to their kind, and trees bearing fruit with seed in them, according to their kind; and God saw that it was good.* **- Genesis 1:12 NASB**

You have the seed of Christ growing on the inside of you. This seed will produce fruit and in that fruit is more seed. Fruit is meant to be enjoyed by others and the seed is meant to be replanted to produce even more. This is not a maybe; this is the nature of Christ in us and through us. Multiplication is the natural result of a heart that has been purified into good soil and the seed of Christ that has been protected from the scheme of the enemy.

> *You will know them by their fruits. Grapes are not gathered from thorn bushes, nor figs from thistles, are they? So every good tree bears good fruit, but the bad tree bears bad fruit. A good tree cannot bear bad fruit, nor can a bad tree bear good fruit. Every tree that does not bear good fruit is cut down and thrown into the fire. So then, you will know them by their fruits.* **- Matthew 7:16-20 NASB2020**

Understand this: a seed will always produce after its own kind. If you sow the seed of Christ, you get more of Christ in the people around you. But what if you withhold the Holy Spirit fruit of your life from others? Isn't the fruit of your life meant to be enjoyed by others? How will they taste and see that God is good? How will they have the seed of Christ planted in them? You must allow the fruit of the Holy Spirit that comes off of your life to be enjoyed and planted in others.

> *For as the earth produces its sprouts, And as a garden causes the things sown in it to spring up, So the Lord God will cause righteousness and praise To spring up before all the nations.* **- Isaiah 61:11 NASB2020**

It's time to multiply:

Exponential Discipleship vs. Conversion Growth

Would you rather have...?
10,000 Disciples Every Year for 30 years (300,000)
Or Disciples Double Every Year for 30 years (5,368,709)

MULTIPLY

John 15: 5 *I am the vine, you are the branches; the one who remains in Me, and I in him bears much fruit, for apart from Me you can do nothing.*

Verse 8 goes on to say... *My Father is glorified by this, that you bear much fruit, and so prove to be My disciples*

The proof of being His disciple is that you bear much fruit. (not some fruit) but a lot of fruit. If we abide in Christ as the vine and we are the branches, how can we not produce abundantly? If the seed of Christ has been planted in you and you have good soil, you will produce a massive harvest with extra seed to sow into other people. You will multiply.

I planted the seed in your hearts, and Apollos watered it, but it was God who made it grow. 7 It's not important who does the planting, or who does the watering. What's important is that God makes the seed grow. 8 The one who plants and the one who waters work together with the same purpose. And both will be rewarded for their own hard work. 9 For we are both God's workers. And you are God's field. You are God's building. **- 1 Corinthians 3:6-9 NLT**

After the seed of Christ has been sown into someone's life, you may water that seed. But you also may not. Someone else may be called to water and cultivate the seed of Christ that came from your life. Ultimately, it is our job to be obedient and continue to sow and water where God tells you. We are all working together for the same harvest. This world is God's field and these people are all His. He is the head farmer and we are His assistants.

Truly, truly I say to you, unless a grain of wheat falls into the earth and dies, it remains alone; but if it dies, it bears much fruit **- John 12:24**

Jesus died so you would bear much fruit.

Now the promises were spoken to Abraham and to his seed. He does not say, "And to seeds," as one would in referring to many, but rather as in referring to one, "And to your seed," that is, Christ. **- Galatians 3:16 NASB**

*He chose to **give** us birth through the word of truth, that **we** might be a kind of **firstfruits** of all he created.* **- James 1:18 NIV**

A TREE OF IT'S OWN KIND

And he showed me a river of the water of life, clear as crystal, coming from the throne of God and of the Lamb, 2 in the middle of its street. On either side of the river was the tree of life, bearing twelve kinds of fruit, yielding its fruit every month; and the leaves of the tree were for the healing of the nations. **- Revelation 22:1-3 NASB**

On either side of the river? The Tree of Life is not a single tree, it's a species of tree. Jesus is the Tree of life. And His seed is now growing in you. On either side of the river means there is an entire grove; an orchard of trees connected by a root system tapped into the River. They bear twelve kinds of fruit twelve months out of the year.

Discussion:

Would you describe yourself as a tree of life?

Who is helping you cultivate the garden of your heart?

ACTIVATION: GET RADICAL

One person gives freely, yet gains even more; another withholds unduly, but comes to poverty. 25 A generous person will prosper; whoever refreshes others will be refreshed. - **Proverbs 11:24-25**

Receiving + Giving = Growing

Radical receivers become radical givers.

Radical givers experience radical growth

Giving is like working out. What makes your muscles sore when you first start working out is not the same weight that will make you sore 6 months later. Giving should not hurt so much that it puts you in the hospital. It should hurt like sore muscles the day or two after you workout.

> *Now He who supplies seed to the sower and bread for food will supply and multiply your seed for sowing and increase the harvest of your righteousness; 11 you will be enriched in everything for all liberality, which through us is producing thanksgiving to God. 12 For the ministry of this service is not only fully supplying the needs of the saints, but is also overflowing through many thanksgivings to God.* - **2 Corinthians 9:10-12 NASB**

Here's how we get radical

"Father, thank you for providing my needs and funding my dreams. How would you like me to be a radical receiver and a faithful giver this season?"

Questions
What does it look like to give in these three areas?

Time _____

Talent _____

Treasure _____

When you think about being radical in your receiving and your giving, what feelings, thoughts or responses are you having?

Has this ministry been a blessing to you?

Become a monthly partner.

Your partnership helps us continue to reach and make disciples through powerful content like this book.

give.arkidentity.com

THE DAILY ID
55 Devotionals written by the ARK Community

Available on Amazon

The Gospel is meant to be experienced in 3D.

Join us for a LIVE event.

3D.arkidentity.com

Made in the USA
Monee, IL
24 April 2025

15948731R00026